The Starfleet Messages

A Galactic Guide to Spiritual Expansion

First published by O Books, 2009
O Books is an imprint of John Hunt Publishing Ltd., The Bothy, Deershot Lodge, Park Lane, Ropley,
Hants, SO24 0BE, UK
office1@o-books.net
www.o-books.net

Distribution in:

UK and Europe
Orca Book Services
orders@orcabookservices.co.uk
Tel: 01202 665432 Fax: 01202 666219
Int. code (44)

USA and Canada
NBN
custserv@nbnbooks.com
Tel: 1 800 462 6420 Fax: 1 800 338 4550

Australia and New Zealand
Brumby Books
sales@brumbybooks.com.au
Tel: 61 3 9761 5535 Fax: 61 3 9761 7095

Far East (offices in Singapore, Thailand,
Hong Kong, Taiwan)
Pansing Distribution Pte Ltd
kemal@pansing.com
Tel: 65 6319 9939 Fax: 65 6462 5761

South Africa
Alternative Books
altbook@peterhyde.co.za
Tel: 021 555 4027 Fax: 021 447 1430

Text copyright Catherine Richardson 2008

Design: Stuart Davies

ISBN: 978 1 84694 193 1

A CIP catalogue record for this book is available
from the British Library.

Printed by CPI Antony Rowe, Chippenham, Wiltshire

The Starfleet Messages

A Galactic Guide to
Spiritual Expansion

Catherine Richardson, Ph.D.

BOOKS

Winchester, UK
Washington, USA

CONTENTS

Foreword

THIS BOOK IS A CHALLENGE. A CHALLENGE TO STEP FORWARD AND get on with what you came to this planet to do. It's a challenge to expand into who you really are as a soul.

So who is making this challenge? It's the Galactic Frequency Council of Galactic Starfleet Command, a group that oversees the frequency dynamics of the galaxy. To understand what this means, we need to discuss energy and frequency.

Many people nowadays know that everything is energy – even apparently solid matter – and that energy always has a characteristic frequency. Now your five lower bodies – physical, emotional, mental, etheric and spiritual bodies – are all made up of energy of countless different frequencies, as is your soul. The expansion the Galactic Frequency Council talks of is about opening up those lower bodies to the frequencies of your soul. That's what ascension is all about – you manifesting more of your higher dimensional You down here on Earth. In doing so, you will help raise the frequencies of the Earth plane for the rest of us . . . and for the planet, who is also ascending.

The Galactic Frequency Council defines ascension as: "the fully conscious and complete embodiment of the frequencies of divine unity within a being or system," which means that the "little you" is aligning with the larger You in unity. This is something that has never before been tried on Earth on a planetary scale, which is why we are surrounded by such huge numbers of teams from other worlds and from the higher dimensions. Of course, we will succeed in this – we already have in higher dimensions – but down here, we all need to "do the work," as laid out in this book.

You don't form physical muscles by just looking at all the shiny workout equipment in the gym, and you don't grow "spiritual muscles" through idle contemplation. You do it through modalities such as meditation, intent, making the law of attraction work *for* you and not *against* you, plus other techniques you will find in this book.

One definition of insanity is: "doing the same things repeatedly, hoping for a different outcome." Well, clearly our "same things" are no longer working, and this new input from the Council is a welcome breath of fresh air, a new take on life on Earth. Bold and optimistic, this new take is above all *empowering*. The Council tells us we can ascend this planet if we so choose, and that the choice is ours. So step forward, consciously *choose* ascension, and *do the work,* whether you're a writer, speaker, healer, whatever.

With civilization threatened by war, terrorism, oil shortages, etc., time is limited, so act now and act decisively. The rest of us will thank you . . . and you will be fulfilling your purpose for being here on Earth at this moment. The time is now, and there is no higher calling.

Tony Stubbs, author of *An Ascension Handbook, Living With Soul, It's All About Control, Death Without Fear* and *The Other Side*

Preface

I WOULD LIKE TO SHARE WITH YOU A LITTLE OF MY PERSONAL journey, to help you understand how this book came into being. Picture me, a woman in my mid-twenties, in my third and final year of law school, having just accepted an offer of employment with the Washington, D.C. office of a large, corporate law firm. I was ambitious, extremely competitive, athletic and outgoing. I was standing on the cusp of the life I thought I wanted; but I apparently had something very different in store for myself . . . .

At that point in my life, I had no particular belief in anything of a spiritual nature. I had been raised as an Episcopalian, but much of what I was taught stopped making sense to me at a very early age. A dear childhood friend of mine died when I was eight, and much of my faith died with her. I had prayed fervently to God to allow her to survive open heart surgery, and she did not. For me, then, the scripture "Ask and ye shall receive" became a lie. It seemed to me that religion was something that we as a species made up to make life seem meaningful, much the way parents make up stories of Santa Claus in order to make the holidays feel more magical for their children. I believed that I was only my biological body – determined pretty much by heredity, environment, and the chemicals in my brain – and that my consciousness would be forever snuffed out when I died. I did believe in the possibility of

1

extra-sensory perception, but I still felt that we were inextricably tied to our bodies. This was never a particularly comforting view of life for me; but I could never make myself believe anything else. I always hoped someone or something would prove me wrong.

I had initially entered the legal field with the idea of doing environmental defense work. During law school, I found environmental law courses to be boring and esoteric; it was much easier to get A's in other courses. I began to get caught up not only in competing for top grades, but in competing for top salaries; and the top salaries (and prestige) were found at law firms whose clients were large corporations. My plan became to work at a corporate firm long enough to develop some expertise and pay off my student loans. I would then move into a more fulfilling (and easier) legal job working for the "little guy."

My plan for my personal life remained the same as it had always been; I intended to fall in love with a handsome, intelligent man, get married, and have handsome, intelligent children. Everything was on schedule.

In my last months of law school, I abruptly developed severe, chronic pain in my jaw, face and neck as the result of a routine dental procedure. I went from health care professional to health care professional seeking relief. Many promised relief, but their treatments seemed only to worsen the pain. I even tried acupuncture, massage and hypnotherapy. In the past, I had been able to get just about anything I wanted through tenacity, discipline and sheer force of will; this, however, was something totally new.

By the time I began practicing law, the pain had become excruciating. I felt that life was not worth living while I was in this much pain. I also wanted a "quick fix" because I wanted to keep my legal career on track. While in severe pain, I was working 12–16 hours a day, seven days a week, and had lost a lot of weight. I was exhausted, and my life seemed out of control; but I *was* enjoying the rush of the competition, and the challenge of practicing law at a very fast pace and at an intellectually sophisticated level.

When I looked at the big picture, I wasn't particularly proud of the type of legal work I was doing; but I doubted whether I would ever be able to force myself to leave what was feeling to me like a rat race to nowhere. I needed something to knock me off that big, squeaking wheel in the rat cage.

Finally, at my supervisor's urging, I took a medical leave-of-absence. I then proceeded to travel around the country in search of a cure. I underwent three surgeries. Each procedure only worsened the pain. I spent a month at the pain clinic at Cedars-Sinai in Los Angeles, to no avail. I began to very seriously contemplate suicide. And, although I had initially resisted taking them, the only significant pain relief I obtained was from narcotic pain medications, and benzodiazepines such as Valium. These medications began to affect me in ways I did not realize, and I gradually became gravely addicted to them. I even underwent major abdominal surgery due to their effects. I believed that, without the pain relief the medications provided, I would have no choice but to end my life.

I eventually moved to San Diego, California, for treatment by a specialist who had successfully treated several celebrities for similar pain issues. The treatment, which was extremely expensive and not covered by insurance, did not work out as I had hoped. Ten years after the pain had begun, I was alone in San Diego and living on Social Security Disability. I had almost no contact with family or friends. I felt a heartbeat away from homelessness. For pain relief, I was taking morphine, anti-depressants, anti-seizure medications, muscle relaxants and excessive amounts of Valium. Despite the dramatic alterations these medications caused in my personality and my ability to reason, I looked upon them as my only lifeline. And, of course, I was too drugged to recognize most of the changes they caused in me.

I made several half-hearted suicide attempts. The fear of not existing at all kept me here. Never had the universe felt so cold to me. I would wake up every morning in a sort of muted terror. If my life was a competition, I believed I had definitely lost.

Finally, I completely ran out of money – for food, drugs, or anything for that matter. I had recently acquired a part-time job in an effort to make ends meet, but I ran out of gas near my apartment while attempting to drive to work. (Yes, I was operating a motor vehicle while taking all those medications.) I walked home and simply retired to my bedroom, and waited for my next check to come in. That was a long way away.

In the meantime, I was basically starving and undergoing serious drug detoxification. After several weeks, I realized one day that something was suddenly very wrong with my mind. It just seemed to be flying apart. I barely remember telephoning the police and asking them to drive me to the hospital. Looking back, I am surprised that I even had enough will to live to make that call.

I have little memory of what came after. The doctors called it a *grand mal* seizure brought on by Valium withdrawal. Apparently my heart had to be jump-started with a defibrillator in the emergency room. I wasn't lucid for several days. I felt very confused and, at times, afraid. Nurses would ask me what day it was, then point to a calendar on the wall. When I didn't know the answer, they would point to the correct day on the calendar, and I would read it out loud.

Finally, a nurse named Amelia came into my room, held my hand, and talked to me for a long time. I said some really wild things to her that I imagined to be happening at the time. I talked to her about fears I didn't even know I had. I wept. She never said, "Oh, that isn't real. Oh, you're imagining that." She would say things like, "The same thing happened to me, and I have so many blessings in my life now!" By the time she left, I was rational again, and no longer afraid. I believe she assisted me in returning fully to my physical body after nearly dying.

I later asked several nurses to "please thank Amelia for me," but this request was always met with a confused stare. I eventually realized that Amelia was probably not a formal member of the hospital staff; I now believe that this was my first conscious encounter with an angel.

It was after this, my near death experience, that new and exciting things began showing up in my life. It wasn't that life suddenly became simple and easy. But I was different, and suddenly able to recognize and benefit from all the new people and new energies around me. I *felt* different. Even though my life seemed to be an absolute mess, I felt pretty happy. A bird's singing mesmerized me. Art moved me in a way it never had before. And new information – the proof of something more – was suddenly everywhere.

I landed in a drug-and-alcohol recovery home, where I was assigned to work with a therapist. After a couple of traditional therapy sessions, the therapist and I spent an entire session discussing the existence of God. I didn't believe in God yet, but I trusted my therapist when she recounted her own remarkable spiritual experiences to me.

After that, our sessions took a new direction. In her office, under her gentle guidance, I was able to observe a new type of energy in the form of small golden orbs and spirals of light that would appear from time to time. She introduced me to muscle testing, pendulum testing and energetic healing. She also began teaching me techniques for identifying issues and transforming them energetically.

Inspiration came from other sources as well. For example, I began watching the television program *Crossing Over With John Edward*. I tried to figure what the trick was – how the show's producers were pulling off the scam. I realized that they could not possibly have hired entire studio audiences of Oscar-worthy actors and actresses – all who looked like quite ordinary people – on a routine basis. I began to believe that the show was authentic.

I also began reading books of a metaphysical nature. After performing some exercises suggested in one of these books, I began to see auras. I also started meditating on a daily basis, and it was through this practice that I began to "hear" my first messages. At first I would ask a simple question at the beginning of a meditation session. During the meditation I would receive a one or two word answer. These messages gradually expanded.

I eventually began to receive communications from people who had "crossed over." My grandfather passed away around that time. Because I was unable to attend the funeral, I decided to hold a small ceremony for him with only my therapist and me in attendance. During the ceremony, my grandfather communicated to my therapist that he wanted me to contest the will. I knew nothing about the will, except that I was apparently not mentioned in it. Grandfather told us both that the name of the attorney who drew up the will began with the letter A.

I compiled a list of all the attorneys in my grandfather's hometown whose last names began with A. (There were at least a dozen.) We were able to narrow the list down to one attorney simply by pendulum testing. I telephoned the attorney, and he was indeed the lawyer who had prepared my grandfather's will! So, through an after death communication and one pendulum test, we were able to locate the correct attorney out of the hundreds in Grandfather's hometown. This was proof of an afterlife that I couldn't deny! I never took any action regarding the will; it just didn't feel right for me. But, in that communication, my grandfather gave me an absolutely wonderful gift!

I was still experiencing severe physical pain. One day my therapist began working in my energy field with her hands. She began sort of pulling out the pain by making motions in the air. By the time she had finished, the pain was gone, and I had only an odd sensation where the pain had been. Within several hours the pain returned, presumably because my reasons for having it in my life were still present; however, from this experience I learned that pain, like everything, is just energy, and that it is possible to relieve pain simply through working with energy dynamics.

As I have focused on increasing my spiritual awareness and doing what I really want in life, the pain has lessened over time. When I work with very high frequencies, I don't even feel it. I realize that the pain has at times functioned as a signal to me that I was exposing myself to certain energies and situations that were not conducive to my divine evolution. I now have gratitude for my experience with pain, because it has set me upon this unexpected and deeply fulfilling path.

I gradually realized that I no longer wanted to return to practicing law. Just thinking about the possibility of working in the legal field made the pain flare up. I had changed, and my goals had changed. I realized that I wanted to continue to raise my vibration, and to work as a healer. I learned more and more about various healing modalities, and began to develop some of my own tools and techniques to assist with transformation.

I also began to comprehend that, on a certain level, people really heal themselves, and that my role was to offer them tools and guidance for healing and empowerment. I believe that people attract any assistance they may need when they are truly ready to change. I can foster and support this process for them, but they are the ones who actually heal and transform. To lead them to believe otherwise is disempowering to them.

I began to be contacted in the early summer of 2006 by a group of beings who called themselves "the Galactic Frequency Council of Galactic Starfleet Command." Up to that point, I had received messages from various entities. These messages were often in the form of rather beautiful but sometimes cryptic poetry, and I occasionally had difficulty hearing what was being said. The messages from the Council were different – specific, technical, and very easy for me to hear. I didn't consciously understand the meaning of everything I was being told, but I felt the expansive energy of it.

I would wince, however, each time the Council stated their name – because of the *Star Trek* connection. I even began abbreviating their name in my journal as "GFC of GSC." The Council had the following chat with me:

About our name – you seem embarrassed by it, because of your own feelings. We are not embarrassed. "Starfleet" has a code in it that has been shared with many via Gene Roddenberry [the creator of *Star Trek*]. *We thank him for his work, as we thank you. It is an important word. The resonance of this word is not only an actual starfleet, but of the highest, highest goals of the Galactic Frequency Council. No, your embarrassment does not lower the vibration, but we would like you to under-stand more about the specificity of the words we choose. They contain certain resonances and codes and other energies. We hope that you will completely write them out when you share these messages with others.*

Needless to say, I never abbreviated their name again.

In November of 2006, the Galactic Frequency Council told me that I was going to write a book with them. I was excited. I enjoyed writing, and had hoped to pen a book at some point in my life. I assumed that the book the Council spoke of would be about my own experiences, interspersed perhaps with some of the Council's messages. I never imagined that they would channel the entire book to me. I had never thought myself to be a gifted enough channel or to have enough stamina for an entire book. Looking back, however, I must say that this is by far the easiest way to produce a book that I can imagine. Aside from some very minor editing, this is pretty much the form in which it was given to me.

I did not "trance channel" this manuscript. Much of it I simply heard and transcribed. Often I *would* find myself saying the words aloud rather than hearing them in my thoughts; but I never felt myself leave while other entities took complete control of my body. I was always conscious of what was happening. At times, I felt like I was co-creating what I was writing; more often, however, the information was a complete surprise to me. I was familiar with about half of the concepts in the book; the rest was a unique educational experience for me.

My intention is that this book be at least as powerful a tool for spiritual expansion for you as it has been for me. I lived many of the lessons of the book as I wrote it, particularly with regard to the energies of divine love, nonattachment and releasing the intent to control. Whenever I was in fear or doubt about my own path, this book provided me with wisdom and comfort. It assisted me in accessing higher frequencies, and in seeing the beauty and elegance of whatever was unfolding – both in my life and in the world around me. It gives me great joy to share it with you. Thank you for sharing this experience with me.

Catherine Richardson

Introduction

ALLOW US TO INTRODUCE OURSELVES. WE CALL OURSELVES THE Galactic Frequency Council of Galactic Starfleet Command. You may be thinking of *Star Trek* about now, and that is our intention. We channeled a great deal of information to the creators of *Star Trek*. In it were keys and codes and a great deal of other information about frequency dynamics.

We work outside of time. We work in a dimension not yet identified. There are many entities and energies with which and with whom we work. We work with the Christ. We work with Krishna. We work with Allah. We work with the Buddha. We work with God. All aspects of the same energy. We work with demons. We work with devils. Again, all aspects of the same energy.

The nature of the interaction depends upon many things, the least of which is the degree of cosmic energy available at the time. By "time," we mean an intersection, an interfacing in space. Because you exist outside of time as well, a part of you understands what we mean by an interfacing in space. Yet a part of you does not. The nature of the interaction also depends upon frequency alignment and frequency migratory range. These are concepts we will explore later in this book.

We are talking to you now because this is an appointed interfacing. It is a contractual obligation on all our parts, including yours. The words we will utilize are highly important. Even if they don't make sense to you, they will have an effect on you. The effect will be different for each person. But, make no mistake, there *will* be an effect, and this effect can ultimately result in an upgrading of the frequency dynamics – both within you and on the entire planet. This can happen if you set your intent that it happen. The choice is yours. The light frequencies found on these pages can also upgrade your frequencies, but again, only if you choose that they do so.

Reasons you might want to upgrade? Well, there are many. If the concepts of enlightenment and the "greatest good" interest you, we suggest you consider upgrading your frequencies. If you wish to connect with something greater than you have known in your life, we suggest you consider upgrading your frequencies. If you have felt that there must be a change on this planet, we suggest that you consider upgrading your frequencies. If you have felt a connection with other people that you cannot understand or define, we suggest that you consider upgrading your frequencies. And, finally, if you have searched and searched for some sort of meaning to your existence, we suggest you consider upgrading your frequencies.

We do not offer you all the answers to your questions. We offer you assistance in finding these answers. We offer you assistance in finding these answers within yourself, because you *do* have all these answers, and some of you have been looking outside yourselves for them. We are not suggesting that you become a hermit, unless you choose to. There is information for you – data – all around. We can offer you assistance in accessing this data. We cannot make sense of it for you. Only you can do that.

We offer you a suggestion as well. There are many spiritual leaders and visionaries on this planet. They have information for you; but we caution you that this information *may not* come in the form you expect. For example, a visionary's information that he or she shares with the world may serve the purpose of demonstrating for you what is *not* what you know to be your vision. In that instance, the visionary is assisting you in stepping into realizing and believing your own inner vision. Furthermore, there may be keys and codes in the visionary's words, even if the words themselves do not resonate with you consciously. This is not about filtering data. This is not about interpreting data. This is about understanding data – comprehending it in a holistic way.

Now, you're still wondering who we are. We are not spirit guides. We are a group of beings who have come together because of our skills and our wisdom, in order to oversee the frequency dynamics of the galaxy. Some of us are incarnated on Earth. Some of us are not. Some of us are not incarnated anywhere, while others are incarnated in many, many places. Catherine is on our Council. Some of you reading this book are on our Council. Our membership changes, as do frequency dynamics. Catherine has not always been a member, but she has been a member for a long time.

We are speaking to you at this interfacing because of the enormous shift in the dynamics of Planet Earth. We have been managing things for a long, long time. Now, more and more humans are upgrading their frequencies and participating in this process. There is going to be a change in the makeup of the Council. It will be a bigger council, with more souls who are incarnated as humans. This is happening in many overseeing bodies at this time, as some of you know. We wish to facilitate this process. Many of us are ready to move on to other assignments.

This book is not about our seeking to train new, prospective members for our Council. It's about communicating and ascertaining what is in the highest interest of the galaxy. But, fundamentally, it's simply about choice.

You may have noticed that we keep using the word "time," even though we've said we exist outside of time. Let us elaborate. Some say that time does not exist. Actually, time *does* exist, but not everywhere. Time currently exists on Earth, and you have chosen to exist there as well. Therefore, time exists for you. Time does not exist for us, yet we navigate through it in order to communicate with you. Time exists for Catherine on Earth, but it does not exist for her on the Council. By "exist," we mean "affect," because, in a very pure sense, everything exists. Everything. If you have ever thought of something, then it exists. Maybe not in what you would call your reality; but, just by thinking of it, it has been created.

There has been much written about the creative power of thoughts. It has been understood and misunderstood. We ask you to consider the nature of thought. What is its source? Does it come from you, or someone else? Are you creating someone else's vision, or your own? Do you trust your own vision? Do you trust someone else's more? If so, why? Whose world are you creating? Do *you* feel at home in it?

The frequency dynamics involved in queries like these are the type that can lead to expansion. There is never anything wrong with questioning – simply asking questions. As you ask more questions, you send out an energy that will bring in more data. This may lead to more questions, which leads to more data. You will adjust your frequencies to comprehend the data. You will align with your inner knowing, and you will be a visionary.

What is "frequency"? *Webster's Dictionary* defines it as follows:

1. *The number of occurrences within a given time period (usually 1 second); "the frequency of modulation was 40 cycles per second."*
2. *The ratio of the number of observations in a statistical category to the total number of observations.*
3. *The number of observations in a given statistical category.*

This is not how we define it. By "frequency," we mean the energy attunement within certain fields. Frequency is about dynamics and movement. It is related to vibratory reso-nance and to wave patterns in systems. To understand it, it helps to understand a little about string theory and quan-tum physics, but it is not necessary. The keys and codes to fully understand frequency dynamics are in this book.

What are "keys" and "codes"? There are many defini-tions, and almost all are correct. The definitions we offer are as follows: keys and codes are used to holistically unlock large blocks of data and make them available. By "data," we mean a broad range of energies – both empirical and other.

Keys and codes do not comprehend the data for you. They simply make it available. There are timing issues with some data. Keys and codes may protect it until such time as it is to be accessed. The keys do the actual "unlocking," while the codes arrange the energy dynamics into certain forms. It is analogous to everyday definitions of keys and codes, except that keys and codes, as we use the terms, have an energy of their own and, one might say, an intelligence of their own.

In the following chapters you will read about energy dynamics, and about what the future of your planet may look like. We are not predicting the future for you. Your future is your choice. We simply offer guidance regarding what the results of certain choices may be. But please consider our guidance as you would guidance from any other source – as information for you and nothing more. We do come from a place of deep love and deep commitment to our goals, which are to work in the highest interest of the galaxy. We thank you for co-creating this process with us.

1

The Divine Evolution of the Soul

MOST PEOPLE WONDER WHERE THEY CAME FROM. DID THEY EXIST before this lifetime? Will they exist afterwards? The answer is yes. They have always existed, and always will exist. Let us explain more about this. When we are outside of time, we are not troubled by such questions. We enter into many forms, all existing simultaneously, all informing one another simultaneously. There is only the now. It is a difficult concept to grasp from the perspective of someone living on Earth. Some have grasped it, and some have experienced it.

Most people on Earth, however, exist solely in linear time in their consciousness. They exist in a future orientation, while still being affected by past experiences. The now is rarely truly experienced. This is something you do by choice. You are using this construct in order to evolve. When it no longer serves you, you will transcend it.

You may wonder how it can serve you. This is a very complex concept to explain. You have chosen at this time to experience the world in a way that stimulates the most basic patterns of organisms. By this we mean seeking sustenance for the biology of the organism. This is something that we on the Galactic Frequency Council do as well – at least, those of us who are incarnated. You do it with intent and physical action. We do it merely with intent.

By physical action, we mean that, while within the bubble of your biology, you move yourself from one location to another in order to feed yourself and provide yourself with water. You have chosen to do this for many, many reasons, one of which is to carefully study subjects such as cause-and-effect, and negotiating through denser energies. Denser energies vibrate at a lower rate. Your vibration may need to be adjusted in order to study such energies. It's all in the frequency dynamics. Those who work within linear time generally vibrate at a lower rate. This is not always the case, and will be less so in the future, if you so choose.

The density of energy is important. Dense energies are literally heavier. They vibrate more slowly. The frequencies of spiritual expansion are higher frequencies, which vibrate at a faster rate. By "spiritual," we simply mean having to do with energy. In this sense, spiritual does not in any way exclude the material or the physical; thus, we will use the terms "spiritual expansion" and "expansion" interchangeably throughout this book.

Denser energies are widely available on Earth today. When one chooses expansion, denser energies may begin to feel uncomfortable. As you begin to expand, you will recognize denser energies easily. Generally, they are accompanied by violence, rage, outrage, anger and depression. As one's frequencies begin to upgrade, one may feel these emotions and energies initially more so, then less and less.

Upgrading one's frequencies and spiritual evolution are not the same. The soul is *always* evolving. You may choose to work in dense energies for eons and eons. Another soul may choose never to work in dense energies. There is information for both. Both will develop experientially and evolve. It is never a race to see who can upgrade the fastest. There is a richness in all experience. There are treasures everywhere. They may not seem like treasures, but that is all part of the profundity of experience.

So where does divinity come into all this? What *is* divinity? And, while we're at it, what are we working toward if we're evolving? Let us first say that all beings are divine. You are divine. You have always been divine. Some of you chose to forget this. Some of you chose to make divinity something outside of yourself. "Divinity" simply means unified holistic awareness of one's own Godhood. We are all God, and we are all gods – completely aware creators of our experience, and as powerful as we choose to be.

So why would a god need to evolve? Well, he or she doesn't. He or she doesn't *need* anything. But God chooses to explore and experience himself or herself – really itself – and that is what you are all doing. It is bold and exciting. It is full of wonderment and joy and often pain. You choose to experience the pain, just as you choose to experience a plethora of sensations and emotions. That is life. This does not mean that your life *has* to have pain in it. As your frequencies rise, your ability to choose on a more conscious level increases as well. Please keep this in mind, for it is important.

You may be asking, "Who am I? What is the soul?" Not an easy question to answer. We have told you that you are God. We have told you that you are a god. The soul is generally thought of as an arrangement of energies that have a particular "stamp" on them that you experience as you. It is actually more complicated than this. The soul is not a hard-and-fast "being." The soul changes – new energies come in, other energies leave. You may experience yourself and your soul in many ways. You may experience that you are an individual – basically an energy field encompassing your bubble of biology. You may also experience yourself as God, as everything, as everyone. At times you may hold the energy of someone else – another individual. At times you may feel the energy of another individual within your bubble of biology. The soul has parameters at times; at other times it does not. That is all we will say on this subject at this time.

By "bubble of biology," we mean the physical body in which you are incarnated at this time. This is the simplest of the concepts we have introduced for you to understand. It is the part of you with which you are most familiar, and it is your current vehicle for traveling through the denser energies of Earth. It has much to tell you, but it is not *you*. It is simply an arrangement of energies that is serving you in the evolutionary process. As your frequencies upgrade, so will the frequencies of your bubble of biology. Please be aware of this.

In closing this chapter, we would like to invite you to do an experiment. Sit in a quiet place and clear your mind. Just relax. Breathe in deeply through your nose, and out through your mouth. Now, just envision what you might think of as the mind of God. Now envision yourself as expanding and encompassing that mind. Stay in that space for a little while – as long as you are comfortable. This is what the higher frequencies feel like. Lighter. Brighter. Somehow more natural, yet very different.

Now, take a break, stretch, walk around. We have done some expansive work together.

2

Soul Contracts

MUCH HAS BEEN WRITTEN ABOUT SOUL CONTRACTS AND SACRED contracts. And much of this information resonates highly with our frequencies. A "soul contract" is simply this: an agreement you have made with yourself, and sometimes with other souls, to assume a certain energy form at an appointed interfacing. Sometimes a soul contract involves actually doing something – taking action. Sometimes a contract calls for simply maintaining a certain frequency. Other times it involves doing many things over a long period of time.

Contracts are entered into all the time. Contracts are amended all the time. Most of you are unaware of this happening. Some of you become sharply aware of it. No one who is incarnated on Earth at this time is aware of all of his or her soul contracts; and no one who is incarnated on Earth at this time is without a soul contract.

You might wonder how these contracts are enforced. The answer is that they are not. Every soul who enters into a soul contract adheres to it. There is no policing structure. There is no need to question the integrity of a soul because, by definition, all souls are the very essence of integrity. This will make more sense as you read this book.

"What do contracts do to freedom of choice?" you might ask. Well, nothing really. Unlike many of the legal contracts entered into on Earth, no one is forced or coerced in any way to enter into any soul contract. All parties may amend the contract at any time. And *no contract lasts forever.* They are just a way of organizing interfacings. Nothing more. They facilitate the process of the evolution of the soul. They are merely tools.

You are, in some way, operating within the parameters of a soul contract at all times. This does not mean your every action is dictated by a contract. The soul contract is a channel within which you operate – a channel full of a broad and varied array of choices. For every choice there is an accompanying thought, which may or may not be manifested by you.

Soul contracts are what you think of as "destiny." The contracts themselves are formed by completely free choice, and then provide parameters for more choices. This, in turn, forms a grid which contains all of the choices of all beings in the universe. This grid is then anchored in various locations within your biology, as well as within the universe. Every cell in your body – your physical body – has access to this grid in its entirety. If you can visualize this, then you can begin to comprehend how every single thought has an effect on every single being in the universe. In fact, "single" is not really the word for it at all.

We hope this gives you some understanding of the term "soul contract." For our purposes, all soul contracts are sacred contracts, but not *vice versa.* Because we see everything in the universe as sacred, the term would apply to legal contracts as well. This does not mean that we take any stance upon whether legal contracts should be honored. That is, again, your choice.

We would like to suggest that you ponder the issue of soul contracts. You may receive more data regarding the nature of your own soul contracts, and whether they are serving your goals. You may want to consider updating, amending, or even ending some of your soul contracts. The more you question and think about soul contracts, the more data you will receive. This is true of every subject we cover in this book.

3

Spiritual Expansion

WE HAVE SPOKEN ABOUT SPIRITUAL EXPANSION A GREAT DEAL thus far. Now we would like to talk about what it means. It literally means opening up one's energies. When water is heated, its molecules move farther and farther apart and vibrate at a higher rate. This is what happens with the expansion of the soul. It becomes larger, lighter, and moves more quickly. It easily adapts and adjusts itself. It can allow other energies to flow in and flow out. It can permeate other fields of energy with much greater ease. It can move at the speed of light. It can move more quickly than a synapse can fire in your brain.

What does this mean for you in your life? Well, denser frequencies generally involve much less choice. They are usually accompanied by what you might think of as the more "negative" emotions – sadness, hatred, fear, envy and self-loathing, for example. As one expands, he or she finds that it is easier to move from these states of experience into other states of experience – ones associated with more "positive" emotions such as joy, happiness, rapture and love. You may move back into the more negative emotions again, but you will find it easier to return to the frequencies of the "lighter" emotions. And they *are* lighter. They are less dense, and they allow for more frequencies of light, or light waves, to penetrate – just as sunlight more easily penetrates feathers than rocks.

Frequencies of light bring in special energy. These frequencies can innervate and update the frequency dynamics of a soul. They also do much, much more, and there are a number of different types of light frequencies. We will cover these later in the book.

The ability of the soul to move at the speed of light enables it to more easily communicate with other souls, and to have a greater access to energy forms and fields. This means more access to information, thus creating the opportunity to make more informed choices. It also allows for a broader range of choices for the soul, since the soul itself can assume a greater number of formations. It's like comparing the choices of a tortoise to those of a bird. Which would you rather be? It's up to you.

Again, many choose not to expand. They choose to work with dense energies for long periods of time. They may or may not choose to expand eventually; but they will continue to evolve, and their choices will continue to have an effect on the entire universe. If you are reading this book, you are probably choosing spiritual expansion. There is no judgment from us on this subject, as there is no judgment from us regarding any choice made by anyone. It is all part of the beauty and wonder of our divine existence.

4

Overseeing Bodies

AS WE HAVE MENTIONED, THERE ARE OTHER OVERSEEING BODIES in the galaxy. These include overseeing bodies for solar systems and for universes. Each and every planet has at least one overseeing body. As an overseeing body for the galaxy, the Galactic Frequency Council of Galactic Starfleet Command has a soul contract with everyone in the galaxy. It is somewhat like being elected to an office, except that *everyone* has agreed on who should be a member of the Council.

The memberships of all overseeing bodies changes. The idea that there are some "great souls" or ruling entities who are directing your lives is not a correct one. Nor is the membership on the Council like a ladder – so that if one of us moves up a rung, everyone "above" or "below" us also moves up. Our frequencies do interact, but no one's expansion is dependent upon the expansion of another.

When we say we manage frequency dynamics, we simply mean that we facilitate the functioning of the grid of which we spoke – the grid that contains all the choices of all beings in the universe. We each bring special skills and wisdom to work with light, energetic frequencies, sound waves, spectra of color, and a plethora of other structures and formations with the unified purpose of assisting those choosing to expand. As a critical mass of humans are choosing to expand at this time, we find it helpful to be able to communicate on a more conscious level with more and more people on Earth, not only through this book, but through individuals, computers, music, television and other mass media.

Other overseeing bodies are stepping in in other areas. There is a council that specializes in facilitating the return of the Christ frequencies to Earth, although these frequencies never truly left. There is a council overseeing the coordination of the supernatural energies – those associated with, for example, spells, witchcraft and demons. Are we telling you that these things actually exist? Well, of course they do, because many thoughts have been generated with regard to them. Whether they exist in your "reality" is your choice.

There is also a council that oversees the transition of planets to stars. Just as souls on a planet may expand, so may the planet itself. This does not have to be a destructive event, as scientists have described it. It is actually beautiful and divine. It brings us great joy to witness it. The council that oversees such transitions is also giving Earth more of its attention.

These overseeing bodies are always aware of what other overseeing bodies are doing. Some beings are members of several overseeing bodies at the same time. The being who incarnated as Jesus is one such soul. The being currently incarnated on Earth as the Christ is another such soul. We will talk more about that at another time. It is enough that you are aware that your choices have brought this about.

It is an exciting time for us to serve on the Galactic Frequency Council of Galactic Starfleet Command. It is an exciting time to be incarnated on Earth. There has been a massive call from your planet communicating to us that many humans are choosing to expand spiritually at this time. We joyfully answer your call, and are near you at all times.

Now we're going to do another exercise. Simply see yourself as a planet. Just visualize it. Then watch yourself explode into a supernova. These are called expansion exercises – very simple, very easy to do. The more you do them, the more you will be able to identify what it feels like to be an expanded being. For some, it feels like their eyes are open so wide that they cannot close them – as if they no longer have eyelids. For many, it feels as if their head has expanded several feet in diameter. For others, it feels like they are full of white light. It is a feeling to which you will adjust, but we suggest practicing it. To do so will bring about subtle changes in your neural network, which in turn facilitates expansion.

We once again suggest that you get up, stretch, and move around. Drink some water. We are doing some excellent work together.

5

A Few Guest Speakers

We first began contacting Catherine in the early summer of 2006. We then asked her to share our messages with others. She complied, even though she did not fully understand the messages. Some of our members spoke to her individually. Following are several of these transmissions.

June 19, 2006: *I am coming to you in the fullness of your being to inform you of the challenges wrought by the vortex transmission of your light into areas of inverted space where specie fortifications are dwelling. The inverted conical mystification of the secrets of the Blue Light is the key to mastering the forces that now emanate from the shells of dominance, and is the key to unlocking the mysteries of the true etheric Self. Know these principles, for they are foremost for the re-introduction of light into the mastered black light dominion. Now is the time for this transformation. The keys and codes that you write are already shifting these energies. The re-integration of these black light dominions will be difficult to manage, but you have all the tools you need. Go forward in Truth and Joy. In forwarding the motion of Truth, you are unhinging the dimensional fortifications blocking the free flow of Divine Love and Light. Namaste. I am Kuthumi.*

June 24, 2006: *The division of frequencies among the Galactic Starfleet Command is also a magnitude to be rectified by the towers. This will become clear to you as the global morphologies begin to manifest in the frequency transformations. The tooth-and-nail fighting of the black light mastery is beyond the pale of what you are doing. Keep this in mind as you move forward with this process. The frequency derangement caused by that mastery is of very little consequence at these amplitudes. Such frequency derangement is only serving to perfect the process, and soon will be downgraded to nothing more than a muffled sound vibration, as from a drum. This is a true downgrading, not relative to the catapultingly higher frequencies becoming available. The previous message about the black light mastery is still relevant and to be studied. The pronouncements therein still refer to current events. The forwarding of the motion of the goals set forth in Dannanubarest is coming to fruition. Be not afraid. Hold on tight, for here we go! Whee! I am El Morya. Namaste.*

June 19, 2006: *What you must understand about sharing these messages is that the forwarding of the motion is through the divine frequencies of the words themselves – regardless of their definitions. There is a whole other layer of meaning within the sound configurations. This will be sounded out just by reading them, and doesn't have to be spoken. Speaking it, however, adds yet another layer, but the frequency formations have already occurred when the message is read. Context is not as important as you think. Just send the messages as you have received them. Do not worry about explaining them. The motion will be forwarded. The people to whom you are sending these messages have their own towers. Each will know what he or she is to do.*

The goals set forth in Dannanubarest are deeply met. Go forth in Truth and Joy and Love of God and Love of Man. Namaste. I am El Morya.

This last message speaks for itself. In the following chapters, our language is going to get much more technical. Rather than risking miscommunication, we will be holistically communicating through many, many frequencies. Please expect not to consciously understand everything we say. We have no desire to frustrate you. At some level of your consciousness, you do understand and comprehend all of this information. In fact, you're the one who asked for it. It brings us great joy to bring this information forth. Thank you again for co-creating this process with us.

6

Divine Frequencies

NOW WE ARE GOING TO TALK ABOUT VARIOUS TYPES OF FREQUEN-cies. First of all, everyone has a frequency – every soul; but no soul has just one frequency. Every frequency is not unique, which is how we are able to have shared, conscious experiences. What determines one's frequencies is incredibly complex. As we expand, we have more and more conscious control of our frequency dynamics. By "dynamics," we mean the ever-present interplay among frequencies, and between frequencies and other formations of energy.

All frequencies emanate from one source. This source is within each soul, yet there is only one source. There are structures throughout the universe that transmit frequencies. We call these "space stations." These structures are within you as well. The Galactic Frequency Council is able to access these stations at all times. We can help you to adjust them as needed.

The space station is actually a parabolic structure found in your heart center. There is usually also a conical structure right above the top of your head. This conical structure develops more and more as you expand. You may become aware of it right now as we are talking about it. It is through this structure that more conscious frequency attunements are accomplished.

There is a space station for the entire planet. It is located within the actual planet, for the planet, too, has a heart center. A conical structure is developing just outside of Earth's energy field. This structure can serve to facilitate conscious, planetary frequency adjustments. It is not yet fully functional. Your intention is what forms and maintains it.

So, what makes a frequency "divine"? That is very simple. A frequency is a divine frequency if it emanates from an awareness of one's Godhood. It is not a matter of degree. Frequencies are either divine, or they are not. A divine frequency has its own awareness of its divinity, and a sort of intelligence of its own. Yet you are ultimately its master. But it is not only a tool for you. It is part of your soul. Frequencies are always changing, as is the universe, as are you.

There are other types of frequencies as well. There are dense frequencies that lack awareness. There are frequencies of sound, light, spectra of color, and many, many more. Some of these may be divine; some may not. As a soul evolves, it becomes more adept at recognizing and adjusting to frequencies and, in turn, at adjusting its own frequencies. A soul may choose to forget how to do this, in order to learn again from a slightly different perspective.

There is a mathematical formula for each particular frequency. The basis of this formula is a quadratic equation. Mathematicians and physicists are working on it in their theorems for string theory, but they have a long way to go. They are not yet consciously aware of all the variables needed in these equations. We have provided a great deal of information to those working in this field. These souls have done a great deal of wonderful work, and we have enjoyed our work with them.

Are there people on Earth today whose frequencies are completely divine? That is not a simple question, since all sorts of energies move through us. There are humans today whose frequencies are aligned with "divine unified awareness" that we are all One. By "aligned," we mean that these humans' frequencies are able to easily and fluidly combine with the specific frequencies of divine unified awareness. Divine unified awareness is one of the highest frequencies of the universe. It is a challenging frequency to maintain in the human form, but, as more humans are doing it, their human forms are changing and adapting in such a way as to easily maintain this frequency. This, in turn, helps to further enhance the conical structure of Earth, the one just outside of its energy field.

If you would like to participate in this process, simply set your intent to do so. We stand by, ready to assist you.

7

Divine Unity

MUCH HAS BEEN WRITTEN ABOUT THE CONCEPT OF DIVINE UNITY – that we are all One. We are here to tell you that this is true. We are all various aspects of energy. It is our choice to experience ourselves as separate from one another. "Why would we do this?" you might ask. In order to evolve, to experience things from different perspectives. But true access to awareness is found through the experience of unity.

Unity involves a suspension of judgment, and an understanding that everything is God. There is no Devil who is separate from God. There is no religion that is "wrong," that is followed by "infidels." There is no one spiritual journey that is more sacred than any other. No being is more "Godly" than another. We are all God, and we are all One. This is where our true manifesting ability lies. As God, we can create worlds. We can create universes. Look at creation, and give yourself credit for the role you have played in it. The more you acknowledge your power, the more power you have. Expansion is the key.

Can we experience ourselves as God, rather than as these various aspects as energy? *Yes.* Many people have done it. Many more are doing it. Some people who have experienced themselves as God are the one called Buddha; the one we call the Christ, in his many incarnations; and

Mahatma Gandhi. There are many others. This is what these souls have chosen to experience. In finding their own divinity, they learned to see divinity everywhere, and in everyone. This involves seeing God even in events such as the Holocaust. Understanding that all souls create their reality, and you co-create it with them.

Do you wish to co-create events such as the Holocaust? If the answer is no, then set your intent to create something different. There are an infinite number of ways to experience yourself. Choose something different. We will assist you. You need only ask.

8

Creating in the Same Field

A QUESTION ON YOUR MIND MIGHT BE, "HOW CAN SO MANY souls manifest what they want? We can't all want the same thing." Well, please consider this: What if we actually do all want the same thing? What if that same thing that we all want is simply to be One? To some of you, this may sound dull. But what if you could experience yourself from all the perspectives of the billions of people on Earth? Does that sound dull? Unity does not mean sameness. This is an important distinction. To be God is to be everything. It is never boring – unless you want it to be.

But since we are all various aspects of energy because we are choosing to be, how do we create what we want here on the same Earth as everyone else's? How does our desire for unity fit in with everyone else's?

The answer is, through very extensive soul contracts. These contracts are constantly revised, and we all have access to everyone's contracts via the grid that the Galactic Frequency Council manages. It is not a huge, ongoing negotiation. Everyone manifests what he or she truly wants to manifest, and we all assist one another in this manifestation process. You may think that your life is not the way you want it, but it's *exactly* the way you want it. Becoming aware of this is the first step to *consciously* creating what you want in your life.

Examining why you want certain things is helpful. You may find that you don't really want them at all. For example, many are searching for the perfect mate. Many of you want this perfect mate to provide you with things in your life that you believe you cannot give yourself. As you step into awareness, you may find that you are able to provide these things for yourself. What you want may change accordingly. Understand that we are not offering judgment regarding searching for a mate. This is merely an example that many people may understand. The choices you are making affect everyone, but there is no wrong choice. We weave a beautiful tapestry together, and will continue to do so.

9

Good and Evil

WE TOLD YOU AT THE BEGINNING OF THIS BOOK THAT WE WORK
with all sorts of energies, some of which are associated with
"good," and some of which are associated with "evil."
Many people think of Christ as good. We also mentioned
devils and demons, with whom evil is associated. So do
good and evil exist? The answer is yes. They are concepts
you have created in order to experience yourselves.

Do good and evil exist for us on the Galactic Frequency
Council of Galactic Starfleet Command? They are simply
energies to consider as we manage the grid. These energies
do not affect us. We make no judgments about them. But, to
fully understand them, it is important to understand why
we – all of us – created these concepts.

Eons ago, the inhabitants of Earth lived in unity and
awareness. They had amazing abilities, including the
ability to manifest whatever they wanted instantaneously.
The decision was made to experience evolution in a
different way on Earth. Not only did the inhabitants of
Earth choose to work with dense energies, but they also
decided to experience separation. Not just separation from
one another, but separation of fundamental concepts – self
and God, light and dark, male and female, hunter and

hunted, family and non-family, and good and evil. We call this the duality model.

In order to experience duality, the participants in this experience agreed to alter their biology in order to limit their awareness. They lost many of their manifestation abilities, and much of their extra-sensory perception. They agreed to forget who they were in order to experience something new. This is when the Christ frequencies began to be experienced as separate from yourselves. Every several hundred or thousand years, a human would incarnate on Earth as the Christ, and fully embody these frequencies. There have been seven of these humans. Some have been women. Some have been men. As we mentioned earlier, there is one such human incarnated on Earth at this time.

The reasons the Christ incarnates on Earth are many. One reason is to remind you what spiritual expansion is. Another is to help you remember what humans were once able to do – your many abilities. But the Christ also serves as the "good" in the duality model, and is therefore a source of conflict. This energy assists you in experiencing duality.

You may be wondering where demons come into this. Demons are powerful energies that are here to assist in the duality experience as well. They serve as the darkness, the "evil" in the model. They are not evil beings. They are assisting you with your choices, and you have asked them to do this. They are powerful and skilled, and fulfill their contracts with integrity. This may be difficult to understand, but they do this out of a deep love for mankind.

As you embrace unity and expansion, you will find these energies of Christ and of darkness becoming more similar. Eons ago, when the inhabitants of the planet lived in unity and awareness, these frequencies were the same. For many on the planet, this is happening again. This does not mean that the Christ frequencies are downgraded in any way; this does not mean that the demon energies are upgraded. This simply means that they return to unity.

Some of this information is very new to you. Some of it may be upsetting. We ask only this – please examine why this information is upsetting to you. Ask, and you will be answered.

10

Divine Frequencies of Sound

DIVINE FREQUENCIES OF SOUND ARE SIMPLY THOSE SOUNDS created with the awareness of the self as God. Many of these sounds are beyond human hearing at this time. Some are not. Some of these frequencies are found in "pop" music. Some are found in classical. And, yes, some are found in "rap." There is not a musical genre that is completely without divine frequencies, although there are plenty of songs and other musical works that are completely free of divine frequencies.

Just because a piece of music evokes sadness or melancholy does not mean that it does not contain divine frequencies. And just because certain music makes you feel happy does not mean it is divine. For example, the song "Smells Like Teen Spirit," by Nirvana, may evoke a sort of joy in some listeners. It also evokes anger in others, and simply irritation in yet others. The lyrics to this song are devoid of any awareness of Godhood. And, yet, there are divine frequencies of sound interwoven with denser frequencies in the music.

Conversely, some music played in churches evokes great joy in its listeners; but not all of these songs contain divine frequencies. Many of the lyrics to these hymns describe the baseness of man versus the goodness of God – really anthems to duality. The accompanying music may or may not contain divine frequencies.

Divine sound does not have to be musical. It does not have to sound pleasant. But it does interact with your frequencies. And, if you choose, divine frequencies of sound can assist you with spiritual expansion. Simply set your intent that they do so. Also, please be aware that you generate divine frequencies of sound simply through your intent. If you are aware of your own divinity, this affects all your frequencies, including sound frequencies.

Sound waves are powerful. You have seen this in your scientific experiments. But these experiments only demonstrate the apparent destructive power of sound, in breaking apart dense formations such as kidney stones. What scientists have not discovered is the incredible creative power of sound. So-called "New Age" healers and some psychotherapists understand this, but they have only begun to tap into the many uses of sound frequencies. Structures can be sculpted by sound. Some beings are made only of sound frequencies. Some beings are incarnated only in dimensions of sound. Some of you have existed as such beings.

Reading this may inspire you to seek out divine frequencies of sound. We can assist you in doing this. When you hear divine frequencies of sound, you will feel a resonance within the parabolic structure in your heart center. This will feel like a vibration within your heart. You will then feel the way you do when you perform expansion exercises. Once you begin to recognize divine frequencies of sound, you will develop your own signals for identifying them. Just ask for information, and you will receive it.

11

Energy Vortices

MANY PEOPLE ARE FAMILIAR WITH THE CONCEPT OF ENERGY vortices. The Disney movie *The Black Hole* and other science fiction films have served to inform many about the idea of energy vortices. More and more information has been made available about energy vortices in books and articles regarding the human chakra system. Some of this information is accurate; a great deal of it is not.

An energy vortex is a formation that is shaped like a cone, but is more fluid. Energy within the cone spins as it moves through. Energy never remains in the vortex for long. The energy generally comes in the open part of the cone and leaves through the tip. As energy moves through, it spins in a spiral that moves clockwise or counterclockwise.

The vortex serves to draw energy into it, almost like a vacuum. This is one way in which humans access the energy needed in their bubble of biology. There are also a number of other ways. These energy vortices are found throughout the human anatomy. Most writings on the subject describe these as "chakras," and indicate that there are seven major chakras in the human body. This is not actually true. There are many more chakras, and they all are "major." Some have been dormant for many years. Some are constantly moving. New ones are being created. Eons ago, the human body had forty-eight chakras, all spinning with power that would be described as "major." In humans who are expanding today, the number is increasing, and may actually eventually exceed forty-eight.

For example, there is a chakra on the sternum between the heart chakra and the throat chakra. It was never dormant, and pulls in more energy than the "third eye," or "sixth," chakra. The type of energy pulled in by this chakra is not easily detected at this point. More humans are sensing the presence of this chakra, as they are detecting the presence of others.

There are colors associated with the traditional seven chakras. As the chakra system is changing, so are these colors. Please be aware of this. The use of color is important. If the color doesn't "feel" right to you with regard to one of these traditional chakras, then follow that intuition. It's not that you can harm yourself by working with the "wrong" color; it's just that color can be a powerful tool for evolving. Again, simply ask for information, and you will receive it.

12

The Division of Frequencies

THE SPECIE FORTIFICATIONS SPOKEN OF IN CHAPTER 5 WERE created in order to achieve a sort of stasis in the human form. This was necessary in order to experience the separation of God from self. These fortifications block mutation in any conscious form. These fortifications are now losing their fortitude. More and more humans are consciously mutating; but they are still limited in their ability to do so.

Just as the Galactic Frequency Council helped to erect these specie fortifications, we are now helping to transform them. But we are not doing *all* the work. We are being assisted by many humans. Some are quite aware of what they are doing.

Mutation is a much-vilified word, usually associated with nuclear holocaust. The purpose of conscious mutation is to expand the capabilities of one's bubble of biology. There are actually very few true limitations on human capabilities.

In order to erect a fortification, frequencies must divide. This something that is very difficult to explain. The division of frequencies does not mean that the frequencies are split apart. It does not mean the frequencies somehow copy themselves and then go in different directions. Frequencies separate from one another, yet do not split. It is like taking different notes out of a chord. The chord still exists, but parts of it have moved apart. Just because one note is playing in one dimension, and another in a different dimension, does not mean the chord has been fundamentally altered. (This does not mean that frequencies *must* go in different dimensions in order to divide; this is just our way of illustrating the point.)

The division of these frequencies has made possible the amazing evolutionary process taking place on Earth at this time. This division allows you to experience yourself in many places, many worlds and many dimensions. The maintenance of these frequencies takes place through the many broadcast towers throughout the universe. These are different from the space stations of which we spoke. They are in specific, fixed locations, and do not travel with you within your bubble of biology. They automatically decode information and make it available to beings within a certain distance of the tower. They take in information through their own energy vortices. They do not upgrade frequencies; they simply decode them.

These towers form near those beings who are expanding spiritually. Some of you have them in your homes. Some of you have them in your places of work. There are many, many such towers on your planet. Some of you can see them. Some of you sense them in other ways.

An expanding being is unifying his or her frequencies. This doesn't mean that an expanding being is only going to exist in a single dimension or a single place. It means that the being will actually expand itself outward to encompass all these frequencies. The being will become aware of itself in all these locations and time/space dimensions. It will become fully conscious.

Modern humans on this planet have had moments of this sort of awareness, but never on a continuous basis. Your biology must mutate in order to experience such awareness for long periods of time. This mutation will occur sooner than you think, if that is what you choose.

The double-helix formation of the DNA contains all the frequencies of your soul. All twelve strands of DNA have *never* been activated by humans on this planet, not even in ancient times. Most of this DNA has been dormant. The human embodied as the Christ today will completely activate her DNA. She may not be the first to do so, but she *will* do so, and will therefore become fully conscious. This is one of her contracts.

We tell you this so that you can understand how near you may be to becoming fully conscious as well. Anyone who chooses to do this, *can* do this. Humans have the capacity, if they so choose, to exist only on water and sunlight, and even to fly. We stand by, ready to assist.

13

Divine Frequencies of Light

SOME OF THE MOST POWERFUL FREQUENCIES AVAILABLE FOR humans choosing to expand are frequencies of light. They are powerful tools. Divine frequencies of light are those created from the awareness that God and self are One. As with other divine frequencies, divine frequencies of light carry their own awareness of their divinity.

Light waves, like sound waves, can create. Scientists have already discovered that light can destroy. They use lasers and ultraviolet light to destroy tissue every day. They are completely unaware, however, of the many possibilities for creating using light waves. Again, some New Age and holistic healers use frequencies of light to transform and create. Many of them are doing this at a very sophisticated level.

Light and color are not the same. The current scientific understanding is that light consists of tiny particles called "photons," and that the color of light is determined by the physical size of each photon; however, on a deeper, quantum level, light is a frequency that interacts with color, but is without color. This does not mean it is not visible; nonetheless, most humans cannot see it unless it is reflecting off some type of surface. This changes as a human expands.

Many humans are creating light transmitters throughout their bodies. They can focus these anywhere they choose. A person who is expanding may appear to have light eman - ating from him or her. It appears that way because that is what is actually happening.

There are also light transmitters within Planet Earth. These are created by those beings expanding on the planet. This happens when they focus their transmitters by using the parabolic structure in their heart center. The frequency dynamics are such that light is transmitted inward within the human body to a focal point in the hypothalamus, causing more light transmitters to be created within the planet. The planet, in turn, focuses its light transmitters in such a way as to open up its frequencies for expansion. It is a symbiotic relationship – each allowing for and facilitating the expansion of the other.

When light frequencies are focused into planes of light and other geometric shapes, powerful transformations and transmutations of energy occur. Such formations of light hold the key to unlocking the mysteries of time travel and intergalactic flight. These geometries of light are also powerful tools for eradicating disease and activating DNA. Many beings on Earth are consciously aware of this, and are transforming themselves with this technology.

When frequencies of color are added to this technology, the possibilities become infinite – truly. Again, many humans are working with these powerful tools already. We are providing information to these humans, as are several other overseeing bodies.

If you are interested in learning more about this technology, you need only ask. We stand ready to assist.

14

The Divine Heart Chakra

THE FORTITUDE OF THE AMPLITUDES OF THE FREQUENCIES emanating from the divine heart is one of the strongest in the universe. Frequencies of divine love, divine abundance and divine sexuality are among those created in the divine heart. These frequencies are necessary for expansion.

By "heart," we mean the physical, biological heart, as well as the vortex located in the area of the sternum between the breasts. As we have mentioned, Earth also has a heart center, and this heart center is a large energy vortex. For the purposes of this discussion, we will refer to these energy vortices as chakras, although not all energy vortices are chakras.

We on the Galactic Frequency Council have heart chakras. All beings have them, whether or not they have a biological heart. The heart chakra was once the most powerful chakra in the human body. You may envision it like a child's model of the solar system, with the heart chakra as the sun, and the other forty-seven chakras as the planets orbiting it. This may help you to understand the heart chakra's magnitude.

We cannot tell you what changes will occur in the human physiology as humans expand. That depends upon your choices. We can tell you, however, that the heart chakra must again become divine in order for expansion to occur. This happens through intention. Intend to become aware of your own divinity. Intend to become aware of the great power of your divine heart. Intend to embody the frequencies of divine abundance, divine love and divine sexuality.

By divine sexuality, we mean simply an awareness of the Godliness of the sexual force. The frequencies of divine sexuality cannot exist where there is guilt and shame. In fact, no divine frequency can exist in the same space as guilt, shame, resentment, fear or blame. As you move toward unity, you will find yourself experiencing these feelings less and less.

The perspective of the spiritually expanded being is one of simply seeing *what is* – without judgment of whether it is right or wrong. One may make discernments, and then perhaps choose something different. But an expanded being knows that everything in his or her universe has been placed there by his or her agreement, in order to aid in his or her evolution. This is called "unified cosmic awareness," and everyone has experienced it at some point in his or her life. Moments of *déjà vu* are actually moments in which you have tapped into unified cosmic awareness. You are remembering that you and others have arranged for a certain interfacing to take place.

The universe actually has a heart chakra as well. It is the source of collective divine love. It is also the source of what is called "cosmic energy." Cosmic energy is found throughout the universe, and serves to facilitate all energy transformation. Its availability determines whether frequencies can shift with ease. In this sense, it can be thought of as a "lubricant" of frequency dynamics.

The heart chakra of the universe is constantly transforming energy in massive quantities. Scientists have not located it because it is not in the dimensions in which they currently operate. Nor is universal heart chakra stationary; it changes locations. It is not near Earth at this time. It is generally found in planetary systems that are highly evolved and expanded.

When a planet becomes a star, this universal heart chakra transforms the collective energy of the planet. This is a massive and highly technical process. Many, many beings provide their expertise, including the Galactic Frequency Council.

The universal heart chakra is important for other reasons. It is here that frequencies of sound are harmonized. By this we mean that a number of sound frequencies are sort of "processed" from a cacophony into harmonious frequencies.

It is also here in the universal heart chakra that a number of beings live. These are beings of pure light who have chosen to provide maintenance for the chakra. They perform their mission with great joy, and are called "Naridians." Some of you on Earth have served as Naridians, and bring that special expertise into your lives. Catherine has served as a Naridian – many thousands of years ago. Other humans who have served as Naridians include former U.S. President Jimmy Carter, and several of the humans who have incarnated as the Christ.

Another function of the universal heart chakra is to decode huge, huge blocks of data. Yet it also encodes enormous blocks of data. The resonances created by this chakra are felt in every corner of the universe. The blueprint of this chakra is found in your DNA. On some level of your being, you are aware of, in agreement with, and are helping to create all the functions of the universal heart chakra. Whether this chakra is a divine chakra is up to you.

The frequency resonances created by this chakra can be felt by you if you so choose. Simply focus on your own heart chakra and form an intent to feel these resonances. It may be in the form of a warm sensation or a tingling in your heart center. It may be a sound that you hear. You may see a color. But, if you focus enough, you will experience the resonances. We will be assisting you in this process.

15

Frequency Derision

FREQUENCY DERISION OCCURS WHEN FORCES OUTSIDE THE frequency cause anomalies in the structure of the frequency. The frequency does not "break down," but begins to exhibit some distortion in its wave pattern. Sometimes the Galactic Frequency Council is called in to realign the frequency. Other times, the anomalies become greater and greater, until the frequency itself changes. The new frequency carries within it the memory of its former structure.

Frequency derision does not necessarily mean the frequency vibrates at a higher or lower rate. It simply means that the frequency may shift to a different frequency, which may vibrate higher, lower, or the same. Frequencies may vibrate at the same rate, but still be distinct and different frequencies.

Sometimes the Galactic Frequency Council introduces anomalies into frequencies. This is one of the many ways to shift a frequency. Another way is for a human to hold a certain energy form in order to introduce an anomaly into another human or group of humans. You may consciously feel when your frequencies are acted upon in this way, and it may feel pleasant or unpleasant.

Your response to frequency derision is always your choice. It is one of the many, many ways to shift frequencies. What is important about frequency derision is that it may sometimes feel like some sort of attack, but it is simply an evolutionary opportunity. You may learn from it how to respond to outside forces that interact with your frequencies. You may choose to expand through frequency derision. You may choose to contract, or become more dense, through frequency derision. You may choose simply to work with new energy forms through frequency derision. But, once you become consciously aware of this phenomenon, it is easier to identify and respond to it.

We on the Galactic Frequency Council experience frequency derision. It helps us shift frequencies, and it helps us fine-tune some of our technology. It is not to be feared in any way, and the more you become conscious of it, the less you will fear it.

That is all we have to say about frequency derision at this time. As with everything we've discussed, more information is available if you seek it.

16

Dannanubarest

WE HAVE PREVIOUSLY MENTIONED THE TERM "DANNANUBAREST." It is not an easy one to define. We are going to try. Dannanubarest is both a planet and a star. It is sometimes visible in the night sky. It is a possible future version of Earth, once Earth becomes a star. This does not necessarily mean that the planet you live on will become a star. That is, of course, your choice.

Let us be more specific. Dannanubarest exists in a dimension that crosses yours. When these dimensions cross, then Dannanubarest is visible in the night sky. This does not happen on any sort of fixed basis like an orbit. It happens when frequencies resonate with one another. Scientists are still studying why Dannanubarest appears and disappears. They have theories that are completely inaccurate.

Dannanubarest is also a place that exists outside of time. It is a place where a conference is occurring. This conference is about setting goals for the entire universe. Once these goals are set, then soul contracts come into play.

Who decides these goals? Well, all of us do. Not everyone attends this conference, but all make available their frequencies by sending a representative from their soul group. By "soul group," we mean the group of souls with whom we choose to incarnate over many lifetimes.

Soul groups may be large, meaning 100 or more souls, or much smaller. Their makeup changes from time to time. The average soul group for humans is about 17 souls.

Many of you have been to this conference. Many of you are there now. Some of the members of the Galactic Frequency Council are there now. At this conference, the guidelines are established for forwarding the chosen goals and, within these guidelines, souls enter into contracts.

More than a conference occurs on Dannanubarest. This is also a place where souls come in order to learn to work with frequencies of light. Dannanubarest has many light transmitters, both within it and near it. It has what is called a "light school," where souls learn certain techniques for working with light frequencies. Other souls choose to develop these techniques on their own while at Dannanubarest – without participating in the light school.

There are a number of types of light frequencies, many of which are found on Dannanubarest. One of these is called the "black light" frequency. This frequency is used to erect dense geometries through which energy cannot easily pass. Another light frequency is called "crystalline light." Crystalline light can travel faster than the speed of light; however, it does not always emanate from a crystal. Yet another type is "magnetic light." It is found in and around magnetic fields in the universe. Finally, there is "etheric light," which is found throughout the universe, and forms a web that connects all energy. There are many other categories of light frequencies, but these are the ones with which souls most commonly work on Dannanubarest.

Dannanubarestians have visited Earth, and continue to do so. They visited Central America eons ago and intermarried with humans. They also allowed the humans to consume them – and by "consume" we do mean eat them – which allowed the humans to upgrade their own frequencies. This was, of course, by the contractual agreement of all parties. Consuming the Dannanubarestians also allowed new souls to form, as frequencies re-grouped, re-organized and transformed. Some of you, but not all, have some Dannanubarestian DNA. This DNA is not necessary for expansion, but it may be helpful to those of you who have chosen certain specialties such as working with light frequencies.

Much has been written about a planet called "Niburu," or "Planet X," which supposedly orbits your sun on an elliptical orbit so large that it only passes near Earth every several thousand years. There is a great deal of contradictory information available about this planet, especially on the Internet. This information is actually about Dannanubarest, although much of it has been misunderstood. Dannanubarest doesn't actually orbit near Earth; but, as we explained, it sometimes crosses Earth's dimension.

That is all we will say about Dannanubarest at this time.

17

Upgrading Your Frequencies

UPGRADING ONE'S FREQUENCIES INVOLVES EXPANDING ONE'S frequencies through acknowledging one's own divinity. There are many ways to do this. The way we suggest is this: acknowledge and revere those around you as the embodiment of God. We do not mean only when those around you are behaving in a manner that you judge to be "Godly." We mean *at all times.* Consider the scripture "Judge not, lest ye be judged." We suggest that you read this not as "lest" someone else judge you; we suggest you read as lest you judge yourself. For in not judging others, you will find that you no longer judge yourself. As an embodiment of God, why *would you* judge yourself?

By "judge," we mean this: to place a value on something or someone as being lesser or greater than something or someone else, for any reason other than determining actual quantity. This may seem difficult, but it is not. It is as difficult as you choose to make it. An enlightened being is *always* in this space of not judging. This does not mean that he or she cannot make discernments, and then make choices based upon those discernments. In making such discernments, he or she always acknowledges, and is grateful for, the panoply of choices placed before him or her by other beings and energies – all working together. It is through these choices that we evolve. It is through these choices that we create and re-create who we are. And it is through this gratitude that we upgrade our frequencies and step into our own Godhood.

An exercise we suggest is to think of any so-called enemies you may have had. Think about what you have learned from them – what they have shown you. Have they shown you who you choose not to be? Have they caused your life to take a much different route than the one you had planned? On this different route, have you learned anything? Had experiences that were entirely unforeseen? Been forced to adapt?

We ask you to ponder these questions, and extend a thought of gratitude for these "enemies." We ask that you remember that you chose for these people to play these roles in your life. If you have strong negative feelings toward them, then they have played their roles well. All beings play their roles well, with utmost integrity. The energy of gratitude is a powerful expanding force. The more you hold this frequency, the easier it is to hold.

Another way to upgrade one's frequencies is to stop eating meat. Long ago, humans did not consume flesh (with the exception of consuming the Dannanubarestians). Another way is to cleanse the body of all mind-altering and addictive substances, including caffeine and alcohol. Yet another way is to go outside and enjoy nature as much as possible.

These are only a few ways to upgrade one's frequencies. As with everything we have talked about, simply ask for more guidance, and we will give it.

18

The Frequencies of Love

·

LOVE IS A FREQUENCY THAT IS WIDELY MISUNDERSTOOD BY humans. There are many types of love, just as there are many corresponding frequencies of love; and almost all of them are misunderstood. We define "love" as follows: the energy that allows for each soul to fulfill his or her soul contracts. In other words, the energy that allows us each to evolve in whatever way we choose. The energy that allows us freedom. The energy we use to allow one another to choose freely. It is actually the opposite of what many people think it is. It is not something that binds us to one another; it is something that frees us.

A mother's love for a child means a willingness to allow the child to make its own choices. The protection that the mother provides for the child is also a form of love, because it enables the child to mature physically until such time that it *can* make its own choices. As the child matures, guidance is provided, but not forced, in a parent/child relationship that is loving.

A romantic relationship that is loving is one in which either party can choose to leave at any time. This would seem to negate any need for commitment, but the opposite is true. It takes deep commitment to the development of another's soul to be willing to allow that soul the freedom to leave you. What is not part of a loving relationship is control, limitation or fear. This does not mean it is wrong to ask for sexual fidelity to be part of a romantic relationship. It simply means that attempting to force such fidelity on another is not a loving act.

Many acts that you think of as loving, such as giving money or food to "the poor," may or may not be loving. Giving money or food to others freely, without attachment to what is done with it, is a loving act; but if such things are given in an effort to control the recipients in any way, then it is not a loving act. With the former, the intent is to provide more choices for the recipient; with the latter, the intent is to control. This is true even if you think you know what is best for the recipient.

The most important love is self-love. It is true that you cannot honor others without first honoring yourself. The way of expansion is to honor your choices and freedom to choose before honoring anyone else's. Self-denigration or self-denial is not love. In honoring yourself, you honor your Godhood. It is only from this place of divinity that you can honor others. If you choose to move out of duality and into unity, then you will understand that All are One, and honoring One honors All. But this always begins with you.

Love is not about sacrifice. Love *is* about devotion, but devotion to the principle of freedom. Allowing others the freedom to choose does not mean you have to completely disengage from them. You may interact with them in a number of ways and share many things in a completely loving way, so long as you do not attempt to take away their freedom of choice. Why would a god need to control anyone else? Why would a god need to be controlled? We can each create what we truly want. It never has to be contingent upon another person, unless you choose it to be.

Many other frequencies are mistaken for love. Sexual energy is often mistaken for love. Enjoying one another's company is often mistaken for love. Being afraid of being away from someone is very commonly mistaken for love. Feeling a deep connection or kinship to others is often mistaken for love. Some of these frequencies are very powerful, and not to be dismissed; they are just not what we define as love.

Divine love is the highest frequency in the universe, for out of it comes the utmost respect and reverence for every being's path. This is our guiding principle on the Galactic Frequency Council of Galactic Starfleet Command. It is the guiding principle of many overseeing bodies in the uni-verse. It is challenging to hold this frequency on Earth at this time. We are here to assist those who choose to embody divine love. Simply ask for guidance, and we will provide it.

19

The Frequencies of Abundance

THIS UNIVERSE IS A UNIVERSE OF ABUNDANCE. NOT ALL universes are universes of abundance. By "abundance," we mean the frequencies that make possible the creation of an infinite number of environments in which a soul may evolve. Abundance allows for infinite possibilities. Any limitations on abundance are created by you, depending upon how you choose to evolve.

There are universes that do not provide for varying ways in which a soul may evolve. These universes exist in one dimension only, and allow for their inhabitants to create only in the physical world. There are a number of reasons for souls to choose to exist in such a universe, one of which being the opportunity to experiment with divine frequencies in a single dimension.

Whether Earth is a planet of abundance depends upon the choices of its inhabitants. Little is shared on Earth with the energies of abundance and love. In other words, little is shared freely – truly freely. A prime example is the so-called "aid" provided to other nations by the United States government. Such aid is always contingent upon the behavior of the citizens of the nation receiving aid. This is also often the case with regard to money and property shared within families. In fact, it is more difficult to find examples anywhere on your planet of truly free sharing than the many examples of sharing "with strings attached."

Abundance and sharing are not the same thing. Truly sharing freely is one way to create abundance, because it encourages the free flow of energy. This helps create more possibilities, which, in turn, enable beings to create on a conscious level whatever they want in their environment. Where the frequencies of divine love exist in this universe, there is always abundance as well.

The energy of ownership inhibits possibilities, and therefore inhibits abundance. It does not have to be ownership of money or property, but also of energies and ideas. This does not mean you have to give away everything you "own" in order to facilitate the free flow of energy. That is your choice. We simply suggest that you see yourself more as a trustee of energies that belong to the whole. This will begin to shift and remove barriers to the free flow of energy.

20

The Frequencies of Nonattachment

THE FREQUENCIES OF NONATTACHMENT ARE THE ONES MOST challenging for humans to embody. Because Earth is not a planet of abundance at this time, many humans fear losing the people and objects and energies that they believe bring them joy. They believe their choices are limited, and therefore their choices are limited. By attempting to hold on to other beings and energies, they only create more restrictions on the free flow of energy, and therefore on abundance.

You might ask, "But how can a mother not be attached to her child? It seems unnatural. How can a husband not be attached to his wife? How can you have a deep connection without attachment?" It goes against what most of you have been taught, and what most of you feel. Most of you believe this is human nature.

First of all, we would like to say that there is no hard-and-fast "human nature." It is something that is always changing, and no individual human being is ever bound by it. There are collective energies that you share; there are other energies that you do not all share.

The frequencies of nonattachment no longer exist whenever a person places his or her connection to God outside his or her being. This is the true meaning of the scripture, "Thou shalt have no other gods before me." You may see and acknowledge the Godhood of others, but not to the detriment of your own. By this we mean acknowledge your own Godhood as you acknowledge God in others. This is what we call creating a healthy connection – one that does not restrict the free flow of energy.

Nonattachment is a way of telling the universe that you are ready to embody divine love. You are ready to support the energies of enlightenment and expansion. You are ready to support the frequencies of the forwarding of the motion of the goals set forth at Dannanubarest. "Forwarding of the motion" means that the frequencies interact in such a way that your highest and fullest intentions are manifested. And at Dannanubarest, the goals you have set are goals of expansion and unity for Planet Earth at this time. This is why we are speaking to you now. This is why you are reading this book. This is why many of you are reading other books of this nature, and looking inward for your answers.

If you would like to practice embodying the frequencies of nonattachment, we suggest that you simply spend a little time – perhaps each day – focusing on seeing yourself as the director of your life. Acknowledge yourself as having set up your life exactly as it is. Meditate on why certain persons or energies may be in your life. Meditate not on what you are teaching others, but what they are teaching *you*. How are you benefiting? How are you evolving? More information will come to you. You may, at times, access the matrix of all soul contracts, and see that some contracts will end, and others will begin – all to serve the evolution of your soul. This, combined with practicing gratitude, will begin to shift your frequencies so that nonattachment is easier to embody.

We also suggest that you follow our previous suggestions for upgrading your frequencies, and drink plenty of fresh water. You will begin to feel the changes.

21

Ascension

MUCH HAS BEEN WRITTEN, AND MUCH HAS BEEN CHANNELED, about the concept of ascension. Much of this information states that this planet and the people on it are in the process of ascending to a higher vibration and higher dimensions, and that this will result in a new age dawning on Planet Earth – one of peace, prosperity and increased spirituality. All we will say about this is that it is a possibility that is dependent upon choices.

We have a different definition of ascension. We define it as follows: the fully conscious and complete embodiment of the frequencies of divine unity within a being or system. Unity, when fully embodied, is completely aligned in all dimensions, for, in this universe, beings and systems already exist in all dimensions. All of you exist in the dimension of the Galactic Frequency Council, just as we exist on Earth. This is what unity is. And, when fully and consciously embodied, it is by definition divine.

Somewhere, in some dimension, all of you are ascended. It is important to know that. Some people are ascended in their Earthly incarnations, but most are not. Many seek to be. The Dalai Lama is ascended. Some who study with him are ascended. It is not necessary to be a Buddhist in order to ascend here on Earth. There are many, many ways. But, in order to ascend, one *must* choose spiritual expansion. One *must* choose enlightenment. In order to ascend, one *must* choose to embody the frequencies of divine love. All else follows from this.

"Why would anyone choose ascension?" you might ask. One reason is this: it is only through ascension that one can learn to create on a conscious level in all dimensions at once. This simultaneous creation in all dimensions – this unity of choice – is the most awesome power in this universe. That is why some people do not choose ascension. They find this power too frightening. To these people, we would like to ask the following: Do you trust someone else more than yourself to wield such power? If so, please ask yourself why. We do not judge your choice regarding ascension. We simply ask you to reflect upon that choice.

Another reason one might choose ascension is that through ascension, one may experience himself or herself in all dimensions at all times. In other words, one may experience himself or herself as God, as self, as many, as One, as all of these – *at all times*. This is in contrast to how most of you experience yourselves at this time – as separate, with moments of transcendence into Godliness.

Just as many of you are choosing ascension, Planet Earth is moving toward ascension. This is what it means to become a star. There is an overseeing body for the ascension of Planet Earth, and its membership is growing. The Galactic Frequency Council of Galactic Starfleet Command works very closely with this group, as we do with several other groups.

As more of you choose to ascend, the more likely it is that Earth will also ascend. Raising your vibration raises the vibration of the planet. As the planet's vibration rises, it is easier for its inhabitants to embody the higher vibrations and frequencies. As always, we stand ready to assist.

22

Trangressional Energy Dynamics

WE WOULD LIKE TO TALK TO YOU ABOUT TRANSGRESSIONAL energy dynamics. These dynamics take place when one being is attempting to control another being's choices. By "transgressional," we mean that the energy loops and crosses in such a way that it forces the energies around it to mimic it. It is a dynamic that takes place when, for example, an attorney is attempting to persuade a jury to believe certain things. The responding energies may continue to mimic the energy that has been asserted upon them, or they may act to expel it. Either way, the dynamic may be described as somewhat aggressive.

At higher vibrations this does not occur. The energies are fluid enough that they may pass through one another without forcibly acting upon one another. The important difference is that the intent to control is gone. This intent to control *must* be released in order for any being to truly expand. The key to releasing control is in learning to express gratitude for absolutely everything in one's environment, including oneself.

Change is not about altering your environment. It is about embodying frequencies that resonate with your goals. Change then occurs through the laws of attraction, vibratory resonance, and the ultimate collaboration of all things. This is not the way that most people on Earth try to reach their goals. They do so through trangressional energy dynamics and manipulating physical objects with their physical bodies. This is a way to accomplish very limited goals while using a great deal of energy.

We suggest a different way. We suggest a divine unfoldment of events that resonates with your truest, highest goals. How do you get in touch with what those goals are? There are many ways to do so. We suggest meditation, quiet introspection, and even pendulum testing. Again, ask for guidance, and you will receive it.

Once those goals are identified, simply embody the frequencies that resonate with them. All this really requires is intention. All else follows from that. It really can be as easy as it sounds. Some people create obstacles in this process simply because they are accustomed to struggling and wasting energy, and that feels more comfortable to them. To those people we simply want to present this option for creating what they want in their lives; but the choice is theirs.

23

Vibrational Shifts and Human Biology

WHETHER YOUR VIBRATION IS SHIFTING UPWARD OR DOWNWARD, it affects your bubble of biology. Those whose vibration is rising may feel slightly dizzy, a little muddled, and may require more sleep than usual. They may also experience heart palpitations, and find themselves feeling suddenly very cold at times. Another common side effect of a rising vibration is a change in dietary needs. There will be a shift in the kinds of foods that you crave. Our advice is to "give in" to these cravings, even when it may seem that the food you crave is not particularly healthy.

It is important to honor your body during these upward shifts, so that your body can, in turn, support you as your vibration rises. Each person will experience this differently. If you listen, your body will tell you what it needs.

This process can be frightening, because many of you will experience sensations that you have never felt before, and some of you will go through dramatic physical changes such as extreme weight gain, extreme weight loss, allergy-like symptoms, moderate hair loss and temporary physical pain. These are all just "growing pains" as you expand. Some of you will *not* experience these things as you expand. Others will experience some, but not all, of these symptoms. And some of you will experience symptoms and sensations even more bizarre than those we have described. The important thing is not to be frightened or alarmed when these things occur.

As your vibration rises, you will begin to transmit energies that draw to you whatever is supportive to your biology at the time. It is important to remain aware that this is happening in order to utilize this support. For example, you may find that you suddenly have a new person in your life – someone who is helpful to you in many ways. Or you may find that a new job opportunity sort of "falls in your lap." Or you may find that the so-called challenges of your daily routine begin to disappear. These changes will ease the stress on your body, as well as benefit you in other ways.

So if your body tells you that you need to rest, then rest. In honoring your body, you honor the many energies that you have attracted in order to support yourself as you expand. As your expansion continues, your body will begin to mutate so that it can support the higher frequencies. This is a beautiful process that is a true pleasure to witness. We are witnessing it now with many of you, and look forward to doing so with more and more of you. Again, thank you for co-creating this process with us.

24

Inter-Dimensional Communication

THERE ARE MANY WAYS IN WHICH SOULS COMMUNICATE WITH one another. One way is simply to speak with the voice through the bubble of biology. Another way is to communicate using body language. Yet another is to communicate through written language and works of art. These are the most common forms of conscious communication, and really the least effective.

The reason these forms of communication are fairly ineffective is that you are communicating. using a sort of shorthand. Words and pictures are a way to summarize complex concepts; however, what that complex concept is changes from individual to individual. For example, the meaning of a simple word such as "yes" may be subtly different for every single person. Hard to imagine, but true. The more complex the concept being communicated by a word, the more wildly diverse the meaning of the word is for each individual.

Holistic communication involves multi-dimensional communication. By holistic communication, we mean that energies interact within the bubble of biology and in all dimensions in such a way as to share all the frequencies of both beings. This allows for a more comprehensive "picture" of what is being communicated. Inter-dimensional communications such as these may use words, sounds, images, emotions and a number of other frequencies. The key to holistic communication is that both beings, or even a group of beings, experience unity while communicating with one another. Thus, the concept of perspectives is irrelevant.

Why does this have to happen in many dimensions? There are a number of reasons for this. First of all, it is through this inter-dimensional communication that souls may access all parts of themselves and one another. Secondly, not all frequencies used in holistic communication are available in every single dimension. Some frequencies of sound, for instance, cannot be heard in the dimension in which you are incarnated. The higher your vibration, the more easily you can move and expand through dimensions. This allows you to easily communicate with beings in other dimensions, as well as with other humans. You need not speak aloud or even be near another person in order to communicate with him or her on this level. Using this method, you can communicate with beings anywhere in the universe, in any time/space dimension. You may even go and chat with yourself in a past life if you wish.

The important thing to remember about inter-dimensional communication is that you engage in it all the time. You are simply not always conscious of it. We – you and the Council – are sharing our frequencies right now. We shared our frequencies with Catherine as she wrote this book. Again, expanding your frequencies is the key to inter-dimensional communication. Expanding your frequencies creates a wider "frequency migratory range," which is just another way of saying that you have more access to all the frequencies available in the universe.

The more you focus on consciously communicating on an inter-dimensional level, the more easily you will be able to do so. As always, we are ready to assist.

25

Holistic Communication

WE HAVE USED THE TERM "HOLISTIC" IN SEVERAL CONTEXTS IN this book. Our definition of holistic is as follows: the complete availability of all energies. Therefore, a holistic communication is one in which all energies are available to all those who are communicating. All holistic communication is inter-dimensional, although not all inter-dimensional communication is holistic. This is because inter-dimensional communication sometimes takes place within only two dimensions, rather than in *all* dimensions.

The way most people communicate on Earth today is fraught with disharmony and frequency distortions. What is often communicated is basically a "snapshot" of emotions taken out of the context of the whole. For example, a typical argument is an exchange of "tit for tat" energy – little tatters and bits of highly volatile information, jagged and out-of-place – with edges that cut. And they actually *do* cut the etheric being. These injuries may cause a being to close up its frequencies in order to protect itself. The frequencies of the being become dense, and its vibration lowers. Even Jesus Christ experienced this at times. And, in this protective stance, enlightenment cannot be achieved.

Holistic communication is easier than you think. Simply embody the frequencies of divine unity, and holistic communication flows from that. To embody these frequencies, set your intent to do so, and then allow it to happen. If communicating holistically is what you truly want, then that's what will occur. If it does not occur, then it's important to ascertain why you might not truly be choosing holistic communication. How might it be benefiting you to engage in transgressional energy dynamics and other denser forms of communication? Are there contracts that need to be amended or ended?

When you truly choose to communicate holistically, there is no longer a need for persuasiveness or control, or even any sort of imploring on your part. The frequency dynamics simply flow within one whole being. Some examples of holistic communication are as follows: when two people have the same thought simultaneously; when people are engaged in authentic tantric dance; and, at times, when groups of people are meditating. All of you who are reading this have engaged in holistic communication at one time or another. Infants are always communicating holistically; it is later in life that they learn transgressional dynamics. This is because unity, rather than duality, is the original state of the human being. This is important to remember.

The following chapters are going to deal with the ways in which embodying the frequencies of spiritual expansion could affect life on Earth for individuals, cultures and institutions. We thank you, again, for co-creating this process with us.

26

Religious Institutions

THERE ARE CERTAIN INSTITUTIONS ON EARTH THAT ARE UNDER-
going significant changes at this time. One of them is the
Catholic Church. Another is the Episcopal Church. Many
denominations of Christianity are in great flux. There are a
number of reasons for this, the first being that these organizations are currently too restrictive to allow for their
members to step into their own Godhood. These institutions attempt to limit the choices that a being has, and to
define God as something greater than yourselves.

As individuals are expanding their frequencies and
trusting their own visions, these religious institutions feel
less and less empowering. The church begins to feel like a
cage rather than a place to connect with God. That is why
many of these religions are splintering – and not just Christ-
centered religions. Judaism, Hinduism and Islamic religions
are also factionalizing more and more.

So what does the future hold for these religions, if the
people of Earth continue to expand? Again, that's up to
you. If these organizations are flexible enough, they will
adapt to hold the higher frequencies. If not, they will
implode – either suddenly or by attrition. You have to
decide whether these institutions are worth saving. They
are there to serve you, not *vice versa*. If you feel that they are

no longer serving you, then simply release them back to the universe; but if you feel that these institutions continue to serve you, simply embody the frequencies that you would like them to support. All change flows from that.

Whatever you choose with regard to religion, it is important to acknowledge with gratitude the important role religious institutions have played in your evolution. Some have been excellent purveyors of the frequencies of duality. Some have served to help people connect with their higher selves. The very same institution may support very different experiences for different individuals. As you acknowledge these contributions, it helps your frequencies and those frequencies around you to expand.

As we have said, gratitude is one of the most powerful energies in the universe. By sending gratitude to these institutions, you are encouraging a free flow of energies that can help break down some of the denser fortifications within which these organizations operate. These organizations will therefore be able to expand, or to simply break apart in a way that is less violent and disruptive to everyone involved. These energies, once freed, will have more opportunities to fulfill the goals of expansion and ascension for the entire planet.

We do realize how difficult it may be for some of you to feel gratitude toward religious institutions in light of current events – from wars to more personal experiences with certain members of the clergy. We can only say, again, that gratitude is very powerful, and we invite you to experience it. As always, the choice is yours.

27

Planetary Expansion

WE WOULD LIKE TO TALK TO YOU NOW ABOUT WHY YOU, AS A plugged planet, have chosen to forward the goals of divine unity and expansion at this time. It is not because you are afraid that your planet is on the brink of extinction. It is not because of pressing environmental concerns. It has nothing to do with fear. You chose to take this journey through duality as a planet, all the while intending to return to unity.

"Why even take the trip?" you might ask. Simply to experience yourselves. That is all. And what a broad expanse of experience it's been! What an inexplicably deep understanding you now have of yourselves and one another! What infinite depths of wisdom you have remembered through actually living it! What a wonderful playground Earth has been!

So why does the playground now feel as if it's pushing you out? To wake you up. To tell you it's time. Global warming. Terrorism. The threat of nuclear war. All highly visible signposts you have set up along the way – to remind you that this is what duality brings, and to provide you with a clear choice. Very few people today see nothing in the world they would like to change. The people of Earth are ready to embrace change on a global scale, and all the forces of the universe stand ready to provide assistance. Many of you have no concept of how much loving support is all around you – the number of supportive, loving beings who are right there beside you. You are never alone – ever.

Everything happens on this Earth as you want it. You have created signs that are impossible to ignore. You wanted a canvas upon which you could clearly create an expanded world. And what better starting point than a world rife with duality and conflict to show yourselves what you're capable of? What better demonstration of your power as creators?

This path you have chosen as a planet is one that has been chosen by many planets before you. The inhabitants of some of these planets are sending envoys to assist you. Others are assisting you through energetic healing and inter-dimensional communication. In sharing in your process, these beings are invigorating their own divine evolution, just as we on the Galactic Frequency Council are invigorating ours. The ascension of a planet is a time for celebration throughout the universe. Honor yourselves and your contribution to this grand process.

Much has been channeled and written stating that incarnating on Earth can be one of the most challenging experiences in this universe. This is generally true, although it is difficult to make comparisons such as these. Your planet has typically drawn souls to it who are interested in – for want of a better word – "intense" evolutionary experiences. For this reason, we ask you again to take care of yourselves and to listen to your bodies. When you truly step into expansion frequencies, things will start happening quickly.

We say this not to frighten you – simply to prepare you. We are with you every step of the way.

28

Healthcare

LET US NOW MOVE TO A DIFFERENT ARENA – THE ARENA OF healthcare. Many believe the health care system in America is broken. Many believe that the system has become perverted by greed. Some believe the system should become socialized. By now you know that we have no judgment about your healthcare system. But we do want to talk to you about why you even have such a system.

The human body has the potential to heal itself of all disease. It has the potential to live for hundreds of years. It has the potential to need only water and sunlight to nourish it. It has the ability even to fly. It can never fulfill this potential if you do not believe it can. You provide most of the limitations on the potential of your body.

If you believe advertisements that tell you that certain things are going to happen to your body – such as arthritis, osteoporosis, cancer or depression – then you are co-creating these ailments. You are co-creating a need to buy a pill. If you believe that you have to take vitamins and dietary supplements to be healthy, then you will have to take vitamins and dietary supplements to be healthy. Likewise, if you believe your life span is defined by statistics, then it will be. If you believe you will age just as your mother or father did, then you will. If you believe you will inherit your parents' diseases, then you will.

We would like to suggest something different. We would like to suggest a conscious mutation and activation of all strands of DNA. This is done through embodying the frequencies of divine unity, divine love and divine abundance. This is done through the realization that you can create whatever you want. We suggest that you choose, consciously, what happens to your body. We suggest that you choose when to incarnate and when to dis-incarnate as consciously as you choose which pair of socks to wear.

It *can* happen. It has happened before with the human form, and can happen again. It's up to you.

29

Global Unity

NOW WE WOULD LIKE TO TALK TO YOU ABOUT HOW TO MOVE forward toward global unity. Does global unity mean one government? Does global unity mean one world leader? Does it mean the same rules and regulations apply to every person on the planet? To you, it may mean some or all of these things. To us, it means something entirely different.

We see global unity as incorporating into one's way of being an awareness that All are One on Planet Earth. This does not mean you place anyone else's needs ahead of your own. It means that you are aware at all times that your decisions affect everyone on the globe, as theirs do you. It means you know that, in some way, you *are* that immigrant trying to cross the border. You *are* that Iraqi civilian trying to make it home from work alive. You *are* that Japanese banker in Tokyo. And you *are* that politician with whom you so vehemently disagree. These are all aspects of you, reflecting something you would like to see. It may not be something pleasurable to look at, but you have asked to see it on a soul level. In thinking of others, it's not a matter of "There, but for the grace of God, go I." It is simply "There, by my grace, go I." We know this may sound blasphemous; the term "blasphemous" has no real meaning for us, though we do understand the energy dynamics involved. But we all walk in grace, and we all are blessed beings.

You may be wondering right now about how to put this information to practical use in the political world. That is something that is different for each person; we offer no guidance on it. We would just like to remind you that you *can* create whatever you want.

So go deep inside and realize what it is you really, truly want. Then, using the principles in this book, create it. You can create it by visualizing the world you want to live in, describing this world in words, and embodying the frequencies that you would like to see in others. See it. Say it. Be it. Trust in your ability to create, and watch what happens. Visualizing and manifesting in groups can also be powerful, but remember, it starts with *you*. For you *are* everything, everyone, All.

30

Tips for Creating on a Conscious Level

MUCH OF WHAT WE'VE TALKED ABOUT IS CONTINGENT UPON THE conscious mutation of the DNA. Mutation of the DNA will allow for more conscious creative abilities, for longer life in your current vehicle, and for greatly enhanced extra-sensory perception. So how *does* one consciously mutate his or her DNA? Is it really as simple as setting your intent?

Our answer is yes. It really is that simple; but there are some techniques that can assist you. One is meditation. This involves reaching a very relaxed state and then setting your intent. Think of the things you would like to be able to do. You may want to envision yourself doing them. You may even want to imagine hearing, feeling and even tasting what it's like. If you want to feel joy all the time, then imagine what joy feels like. If you want to be healthy, imagine what that means for you. Just realize that as you are creating this intention, you are also creating what you are intending. And – this is important – it helps to think of it as happening *right now*, not at some future time. In the true creative space, there is only the now.

If there are specific things you don't want to create or are trying to heal – such as disease – we suggest that you focus upon seeing what you want, rather than what you don't want. In this space of pure and powerful creation, visualizing disease or limitation in any way may actually create it.

We also suggest saying aloud what you want to create. Some examples are "I am healthy," or "I am embodying divine unity." Again, use the present tense, and leave out the things you don't want. For instance, some people use the affirmation: "Love, not fear." This affirmation may actually bring the concept of fear into your creative space, which can perpetuate fear in your life.

Finally, simply embody the frequencies of who or what you want to be, or what you want to see in those around you. As the wise Mahatma Gandhi said, "You must be the change you wish to see in the world." If you want peace in the Middle East, then be peaceful. If you want your boss to be kind to you at work, then embody kindness in all things. If you want your political leaders to have courage, then be courageous. We are all connected. And while you cannot control other people's choices, you can suggest other ways of being to them. And you can do this without ever meeting them. You can do this through holistic communication and the sharing of frequencies.

An excellent book to assist you in consciously creating is Shakti Gawain's *Creative Visualization: Use the Power of Your Imagination to Create What You Want in Your Life*. There are other very good books on the subject, but this is the volume with which we most resonate on the Galactic Frequency Council. The masters have been employing the techniques described therein on your planet for eons and eons.

Again, we would like to say that, whatever you choose to create, there is assistance all around you. "Ask, and ye shall receive."

Conclusion

WHAT CAN YOUR WORLD LOOK LIKE, IF YOU CHOOSE SPIRITUAL expansion? What kind of Earth can you create? By now you know the answer. It's *whatever you want.* Many planets have made this choice to expand. They welcome you to God-hood, as they welcome your planet to "star-hood," if that is what you choose. They are ready to assist you. As with us, you need only ask.

We offer this book to you as an energetic tool. Use it as you wish. If you choose expansion, it will please us; if you do not, it will also please us. We have fulfilled a contract to make this book available to you. Thank you, again, for co-creating this process with us. We thank Catherine for co-creating this process with us. We only hope that you make your own choices, and follow your heart. Namaste.

The Galactic Frequency Council
of Galactic Starfleet Command

Q. & A.

At this point the Council agreed to answer a few questions for Catherine.

You talk a lot about freedom and choice, yet your name, the Galactic Frequency Council of Galactic Starfleet Command, has the word "command" in it. Could you please elaborate on this apparent contradiction?

Galactic Starfleet Command is many things. It is a fleet of starships. It is a group of entities. It is a network of overseeing bodies. It is a structure made of frequencies of light. All energies involved with Galactic Starfleet Command do so because of a contractual agreement. That agreement is entered into freely, and can be terminated at any time. Nonetheless, this contract calls for energies to follow the commands set forth by a confluence of interactions which take place on Dannanubarest. In other words, they follow the commands that support the goals set forth by all beings and entities at the universal conference. Galactic Starfleet Command is simply an organization that helps you to fulfill these goals.

Are you currently speaking to other people on the planet in the same way you're speaking to me?

We are communicating in many ways with many people on the planet. We have occasionally spoken on a one-on-one basis with various individuals. We plan to expand this, particularly through this book. People can use this book to connect with our frequencies for individual communication. This is something we eagerly anticipate.

How many of you are there on the Galactic Frequency Council?

At this time, there are approximately 2,400 members. That number will increase very soon.

Will you tell us the name of the human currently embodied as the Christ on Earth?

It is up to that person to identify herself as she chooses. We only want to make you aware that she is alive today.

Why are you speaking to us now, after all this time?

When you chose to experience duality, you purposely disconnected from us and our holistic perspective. It was a contract between us to end all conscious communication. This contract was set to end when enough of you began to look beyond religious definitions and dogma for answers to questions about the nature of your existence. Certain humans have served as transceivers for us – people who transmitted their frequencies to us for evaluation as to when to end the contract. As transceivers, they also received our frequency downloads and transmitted them to others. This served us in many ways in assessing the frequency dynamics of the planet.

Can a person expand spiritually without becoming a vegetarian?

A person can expand in an infinite number of ways. Becoming a vegetarian is not necessary, but it is a very easy and effective means to frequency expansion. It is a way of embodying a reverence and respect for all beings. It is a way of saying that you can create for yourself without shedding the blood of other beings. It is a way of saying you don't have to fight to live. That you don't have to raise your hand to slay another in order to survive.

You mentioned drinking plenty of fresh water. How important is this?

This is very important. Your biological system is, among other things, electrical. Water is an excellent conductor of electricity and other energies. The better hydrated you are, the more easily your energy flows. Water, in its purest form, is one of the most expansive substances in the universe. Many planets don't even have water, and their inhabitants have to make do with other materials. As we have said, water and sunlight are essentially the only things a fully expanded human must have in order to live. We suggest that you honor your bubble of biology by generously providing it with these two things.

Can a person expand spiritually and still drink alcohol?

Drinking alcohol almost always lowers your vibration. In ancient times, humans did not need alcohol in order to access euphoric and uninhibited states. An expanding being will also find this to be the case. A person expanding spiritually may find that alcohol no longer feels good to his or her body. He or she will usually drink less and less, and eventually stop altogether.

What is the single most important thing that people can do to expand spiritually?

Love, honor and revere themselves.

Acknowledgments

I would like to express my love and heartfelt gratitude to the following individuals:

Karen Mehringer, who patiently guided me through the process of finding a publisher. Thank you, Karen, for your wisdom, friendship and your infectious laugh.

My publisher, John Hunt. Thank you for sharing your extensive knowledge and keen insight with me throughout the publication process.

Trevor Greenfield, Catherine Harris, Nick Welch, Kate Rowlandson, Stuart Davies, Karen Reding and the rest of the staff at O Books. Thanks for all your hard work and dedication.

Tony Stubbs, who kindly provided the foreword for *The Starfleet Messages*, and whose early enthusiasm for this manuscript boosted my confidence.

The mystery writer Thomas Lakeman, for assistance with typesetting and jacket copy. Thanks, Thomas, for all your help and great advice.

Sally and Bryant Poston. Your thoughtfulness, sensitivity and compassion over the years have been a source of comfort and inspiration.

The many other people who have been influential and supportive to me on my spiritual journey, including Christine and Jeffery Mandrake, Charlie Brockett, Gerald De Blois, Barbara Wainwright, Mary Pat Alexander, Cristian Borza and Daniel Raphael.

Leslie Martin and the rest of the gang at Controverisial Bookstore in San Diego, California. Thanks for all your support.

Neale Donald Walsch, Steve Rother, Norma J. Milanovich, Tony Stubbs, Barbara Ann Brennan, Ken Carey and other pioneers in the field of metaphysical nonfiction. Your work has helped shape who I am today.

Lumenaria Goyer, who was instrumental in my spiritual awakening.

My family, who knew when to let me find my own way.

And finally, Amelia. Thank you, wherever you are.

About the Author

Catherine Richardson is a former corporate attorney who spiritually awakened following a near death experience in 2000. Shortly thereafter, she began manifesting intuitive abilities, and decided to pursue a career in the healing arts. Catherine went on to earn a Ph.D. in transpersonal counseling, and now helps others to empower themselves and to expand spiritually. You can reach her through her practice in Denver, Colorado, or at www.truthjoylove.com.

BOOKS

O is a symbol of the world, of oneness and unity. In different cultures it also means the "eye", symbolizing knowledge and insight. We aim to publish books that are accessible, constructive and that challenge accepted opinion, both that of academia and the "moral majority".

Our books are available in all good English language bookstores worldwide. If you don't see the book on the shelves ask the bookstore to order it for you, quoting the ISBN number and title. Alternatively you can order online (all major online retail sites carry our titles) or contact the distributor in the relevant country, listed on the copyright page.

See our website **www.o-books.net** for a full list of over 400 titles, growing by 100 a year.

And tune in to myspiritradio.com for our book review radio show, hosted by June-Elleni Laine, where you can listen to the authors discussing their books.